the

Rouault
The Great Draughtsmen

Rouault

Waldemar George
Geneviève Nouaille-Rouault

Pall Mall Press   London

Rouault
Translated by Noël Lindsay

General Editor
Henri Scrépel
Originally published in French under the title
l'Univers de Rouault, *in the series* Les Carnets de Dessins

Pall Mall Press Ltd.,
5 Cromwell Place, London SW7
First published in Great Britain in 1971
ISBN 0 269 02795 5

Printed in France.

Rouault

Sketch for Self Portrait

Georges Rouault studio

Contents

I

Genius and Destiny of Rouault

Affiliation and Affinities

Rouault gives painting a new dimension. How does he achieve this? If Matisse accords full autonomy to colour, if Picasso pioneers a new perspective during the opening years of the twentieth century, Rouault shatters contours and unleashes a cyclone of tones which breathe fire. His violence surpasses that of Mathis Grünewald, of Goya, of Van Gogh, of Edward Munch, of Ensor and of Kokoschka, of Soutine and of Nolde. But, without repudiating the capital conquests of contemporary art, he turns away from the Fauves and the Cubists. He owes them nothing. He follows a third way. An artist beyond all measure, he can do as he pleases. He has every audacity.

Rouault is the only painter since Delacroix whose affinities and spiritual and intellectual contacts stand out in the full light of day. But whereas the master of the *Crusaders* draws his inspiration from mythology, from ancient history, from modern history and from poetry, Rouault, far from being a "literary" painter, invents his characters. His people are eternal types, like those of Rabelais, of Mathurin Régnier, of Scarron, of Molière, of Lesage, of Fernand Crommelynck and of Jarry. They join hands with Pathelin and Panurge, Tartuffe and Harpagon, the incarnation of avarice, and Gil Blas, the student who starts as thief and lackey to become the confidential friend of ministers, with the Cocu Magnifique and Ubu...

Nude with raised arms (1907)   Watercolour and pastel
Musée d'Art Moderne, City of Paris

Rouault unites the comic with the sublime and with the sense of the sacred, about which we shall have more to say below. His models might equally be the anonymous authors of the satirical farces of the later middle ages and Agrippa d'Aubigné. Biblical prophet and jester, this painter of genius combines a tumultuous and apocalyptic style with frank and outspoken language. He lays down the law. His indictments inevitably remind us of the irreverent gibes of those satirists who had the least respect for the conventions. But Rouault the rebel is also the younger brother of the Roman imagists of Nohan-Vic, of the carvers of Gothic corbels and gargoyles and the sculptors of Fraisé, those worm-eaten bodies. As a visionary, he takes his place in the tradition of the mediaeval miracle plays and the secular mystery plays. He has all the verve of the old jongleurs, whose tales and monologues, whose games and disputes he so admires. His work embraces the farces and the joyful sermons which delighted the Confraternity of the Carefree. Donning a fool's cap, or the skullcap of a hospital doctor, he identifies himself with the roles he interprets. Like the wandering players who decked out their costumes with the symbols of a public office or a condition of life, he presumes that the whole of society is made up of buffoons, whose burlesque dunce's cap will serve to protect them from wrath and persecution.

Rouault bears the same relation to Daumier that Robert Macaire does to Panurge, or Pathelin to the heroes of the *Fourberies de Scapin* or Villon to Rutebeuf. Like the poet of the *Petit Testament* and the *Grand Testament*, he could say, "I smile through my tears".

Villon, the well-read but vagabond scholar, the heir of the wandering players, the mountebanks and the thimble-riggers, even foreshadows some of his writing in his *Ballade*:

> The rain has cleansed you and laved you,
> The sun has dried you and blackened you,
> The ravens have picked out your eyes,
> And plucked your beard and brows.
> All our lives we have never rested,
> Blown hither and thither as the wind changes,
> And at its pleasure unceasingly harries us,
> Never homekeepers, but wild birds on the wing.
> Shun, then, our brotherhood,
> But pray God that we may be absolved of all.

Rouault is a rebellious spirit, whose sources go back to the *Roman de Renard*, which celebrates the revenge of the humble over the great and powerful ones of this world.

He belongs to the line of French pamphleteers from Rabelais to Molière. No doubt his Pantagruelism is questionable, and must be taken with a grain of salt. But he sometimes adopts the drollest Rabelaisian phrases. Terms such as *sorbonists, sorbonagres, sorbonacles*, might well be of his coinage! The astrologer Her Tripa, the mute Nazdecabre and the buffoon Triboulet might also form part of his repertory. Their names or their nicknames bear the imprint of his caustic genius.

Rabelais denounces the rapacious burgess, the begging monk hawking his relics, papal policy, criminal justice and civil justice. Molière castigates egotism, snobbery, sham, hypochondria

Bathers
(1903)
Watercolour and gouache
Private collection

Entracte (about 1906)
Ink, watercolour and pastel
Private collection

and greed, quackery and hypocrisy. All the bigots are against him. His usual instrument is burlesque, but his approach is that of a moralist and even of a philosopher.

The puppets which dance to Rouault's strings, and whose fantastic parade he stages, join hands with the tradition of Mathurin Régnier's briefless barristers, down-at-heel poets and hangers on. They are in the direct lineage of Gil Blas, who peddles his good offices and knows a thousand ways of making money.

It has been said of Rabelais that he found everything good and rejected nothing as being too trivial for his attention. Rouault is no more of a purist than Rabelais. But his pictorial and verbal licence have a prodigious virulence and force. His vocabulary, like that of Rabelais, is enamelled with country proverbs and loaded with archaisms borrowed from provincial dialect. His humour is enormous. Each of his sarcasms is a poisoned barb. He pillories the venal magistrate, the generals armed with wooden swords, and the slave traders. The accents of *Les Tragiques* are found again in his *Miserere*. "God finds the walls of the Law Courts built with the bones of the dead, cemented with the ashes of the burned and the blood of the murdered." These lines and those in which the untamed Agrippa d'Aubigné evokes "the fires which the executioners light beneath the stake, the branding-irons which the victims withdraw from the furnace, a sky reeking with blood and the tortured with their wounded lungs" might bear the signature of the humble and colossal Rouault, the painter of charnel-houses, of macabre sarabands, of the waltz of skeletons, the games of massacre, the triumph of death and the last judgement.

Rouault, a child of the people, remained a man of the people. But, with all respect to his historiographers, Lautrec, a child of the aristocracy, was just as much a man of the people as Rouault!

The living art of Rouault contrasts with the sophisticated art of some of his peers, just as the Gallic and jocular spirit of the fables, proverbs and popular tales contrasts with the chivalrous, epic and feudal spirit of the courtly romances and *chansons de geste*.

Like Rabelais, and unlike Oscar Wilde, Rouault put all his genius into his work. His life will never furnish the ideal subject for an adventure story.

Rouault kept a cool head, even though he pulled the strings of the puppets represented by statesmen, financial magnates convicted of usury, bankers with bowels of gold, pettifogging and prevaricating judges, the whole tribe of robbers and highwaymen. His art made up for the even tenor of his life. Outside his work, his most famous exploit was the holocaust of 5 November 1948. Regarding them as unfinished (none of them was signed) and feeling far too old to put the finishing touches to them, Rouault, in the presence of an official witness and the newsreel cameramen, destroyed 315 of this pictures. His family bequeathed several hundred works of art to French museums, on certain conditions. Two hundred were shown at the Louvre from June to November, 1964. They filled part of the Grande Galerie, the Salle de Sept Mètres, the Salle Duchâtel and the Salon Carré.

Rouault's act is unprecedented in the annals of art. But this evidence of pure integrity nevertheless raises the ambiguous problem of *what is finished* and *what is not*. Are Rouault's unfinished pictures mere sketches and studies? They are in the same category as the *Grandes Baigneuses* of the Cézanne in the National Gallery, London (formerly in the Pellerin Collection) and in the Barnes Foundation at Merion near Philadelphia (formerly in the Ambroise Vollard collection).

Unquiet Adolescence

Rouault was not trained under the sign of the Impressionists, nor did he win his spurs in the wake of academic art. His spiritual father was to be Gustave Moreau, His fellow disciples included Matisse, Marquet, René Piot, Milcendeau...

Gustave Moreau is a marginal master. Literary men and poets admire him! Degas jokes about his Olympian gods "wearing watchchains". The art of the painter of *Orpheus* and of *Jason* is a base alloy of the spirit of Leonardo da Vinci and the Parnassian spirit, the spirit of *Les Trophées* and of *Poèmes Barbares*, of esoterics and stylistics, of decadent aestheticism and of mania for the antique. That, at least, is how he was assessed by the historians of modern painting, whose judgment seemed irreversible. But this verdict has been quashed. The Gustave Moreau exhibition at the Louvre was a revelation for some of the younger generation. If it was only the surrealist painters and a few other members of André Breton's group who unreservedly accepted the *Young Man and Death*, a hermetic work of obscure symbolism, and spoke in praise of *Ulysses*, everyone was bound to recognize that the watercolours and sketches of the hermit of the rue de La Rochefoucauld constituted an anticipation and a premonition. Their rhythms of coloured values foreshadowed the pictorial licence of lyric abstraction! So changeful is the glory of this world!

Gustave Moreau, magician and jewelsmith, whose treatment is all enamel and cameo, was for the young Georges Rouault what Bakst, the creator of fairy *décors* of Persian and Cretan inspiration, was for Chagall when he first arrived from provincial Vitebsk. Bakst went with Chagall to the Hermitage. He talked to him about Paris. He cited Cézanne and Gauguin, Georges Seurat and Van Gogh. Moreau reacted against the mediocrity of school teaching, whose aim was a naturalism nearer to Bastien-Lepage than to Courbet. When he took his pupils to the Museum he was not content with making them discover the old masters. He taught them how to look at pictures and how to read them. If he scrutinized the works of Leonardo, whose genius attracted him, he brought his listeners face to face with the images of Paolo Uccello and Andrea Mantegna. He lingered before the works of Eugène Delacroix. He spoke to his pupils of Édouard Manet and of Lautrec.

Prostitute before a mirror (No. 1)
Watercolour (1906)

Musée National d'Art Moderne
Paris

Odalisque (1907)
Watercolour

Kunstmuseum, Basle

Painting, as he conceived it, is not a projection of reality. It is a source of escape, a casement opening on to the world of dreams, a fiction and a compensation.

Moreau threw his library open to the young man, who was one day to be the curator of his Paris house, converted into the Gustave Moreau Museum, and guided him in his reading. Like Delacroix, Rouault was a passionate reader of Shakespeare. *Les Fleurs du Mal* was his bedside book, as well as the *Petits Poèmes en prose*.

As for Moreau's direct influence on the prentice painter, it was not decisive. While it is manifest in *Stella Matutina* (1895), which derives from a *Hérodias* of the master, or even in *Coriolanus* (1894), works such as the *Road to Calvary* (1891) or the *Prodigal Son* (1897) bear the stamp of an unquestionable Christian spirituality.

No doubt the harmonies of yellow ochres and purples in a picture such as *The Child Jesus among the Doctors* (1894) recall the harmonies in red and gold dear to Gustave Moreau. But a sketch for this work displays a new and original graphic style of extreme freedom.

The Rouault who takes his first steps in art is not a painter after the style of Leonardo, or a legitimate heir of Moreau. He turns rather towards Rembrandt. The drawing for *Jesus among the Doctors* has the broad and irregular texture of the pen sketches of the Bathsheba master. The line is discontinuous. The central motif is suggested rather than figured. It emerges from a tissue of scratches.

Gustave Moreau is not a chiaroscuro painter. His tones fuse before they burst into flame. The young Rouault seems dedicated to monochrome. Some of his pictures are traced in charcoal. Were his researches guided by some of the states of Rembrandt's etchings? In the *Disciples at Emmaus* (1899) he suggests an interior. The *Self-Portrait* (1895) is a burning-mirror. The painter's face, that star of life, is a zone of light outlined in black. It is irradiated by a lost look. This likeness of the artist by himself, wrapped in a greatcoat, is a body actuated by the springs of the spirit.

Rouault is generally regarded as a figure painter. His personality primarily asserted itself in a series of small drawings: *Head* (1900), *Face to Face* (1900), *Judges* (1901). But these drawings are few in number. Strange as it may seem, it was in his landscapes that he first gave the full measure of his unique vision. These landscapes are major works.

Did the artist have in mind the fantastic nature pictures of Rembrandt (and of Seghers) when he painted *Night* (1897) and *Nocturne* (1900), scenes perceived in depth, in which a cold light pierces the shadows? The trees and houses are indicated as summarily as in some of the drawings of Jean François Millet's black style. Rouault no longer bears any traces of a conventional or a timorous painter. He makes use of effects of contrast, the logical consequences of which were drawn by Seurat.

Other landscapes dating from this period are perhaps even more surprising. One example is the *Chantier*, where horses and human figures blend into each other and merge with the natural background looming over them (1897). Another is *Paris*, painted at the age of twenty, where the figures are little more than silhouettes (1891). Its structure is unusual. The arch of the bridge breaks the composition. Like Hokusai, and like Utamaro, but like Degas, too, Rouault records his motif as it inscribes itself in his field of vision. Together with Bonnard and Vuillard he exploits a fortuitous grouping.

The Painter of Virtues and Vices

The theory that around 1902 a radical break occurred in Rouault's work is accepted by all his biographers. But the facts are much more subtle. Was there a deliberate break, or was there a speeding-up of a slow process which had already begun in the years of School and of apprenticeship in the studio of the great initiate, Gustave Moreau? Georges Charensol, in his book *Georges Rouault* (Les Quatre Chemins, Paris, 1926), reports the following account, given to him by the artist himself:

"When Gustave Moreau died, many of us found ourselves in a terrible situation. Matisse, too, suffered a great deal at that time, and so did many others! If my art is harsh, it is no doubt owing to this period in my life. That was when I first understood what Cézanne meant when he said 'How frightening life is!'

"My feelings at Moreau's death were heart-rending, but after being completely overwhelmed at first, I was not long in reacting, and it was an extremely profound inner change. I had just won a medal at the Salon and I could have built up a very comfortable position in official circles; I also had steady contacts with Moreau's admirers.

"But you have to suffer and see for yourself, my master used to say, and it was no merit of mine to do so; there was nothing else I could do. Without deliberately wanting to forget all I had loved in the museums, I was gradually carried away by a more objective vision.

"On fine spring days, before going to the studio, I sometimes used to go, at five in the morning, to paint under the bridges, on the banks of the Seine, near the Quai des Tournelles, where porters stripped to the waist used to unload the barges.

At the Tabarin (le Chahut)
1905

Watercolour and pastel

Musée d'Art Moderne
City of Paris

"It was then that I passed through a most violent moral crisis. I experienced things that cannot be put into words. And I set about doing painting of an outrageous lyricism which disconcerted everybody.

"I nevertheless sent these paintings to the Salon. I seem to have been quite unconscious, and I did not understand my own evolution until I read an article which said 'There was a Rouault who was a serious painter, but there is another who is a poseur'; it was my detractors who made me understand what I had done, but I would have liked to have told them, if they had not been so convinced they were right, that it was not the influence of Lautrec or Degas or the moderns which had inspired me to make this instinctive movement and to change my course, but an inner need, and the perhaps unconscious desire not to fall back in the long run on conventional religious subjects.

"For many years I wonder how I lived. Everybody dropped me, in spite of elegant, but vain, protests. People even wrote me letters of abuse. That was the time to remember the words of my master; 'Thank heaven that you are not successful, at least until as late as possible. That way you can express yourself more completely, and without constraint.'

"But when I looked at some of my pictures, I asked myself, 'Was it really I who painted that? Can it be true? It is frightening, what I have done.' "

The crisis to which Rouault refers was not, apparently, an aesthetic conflict. It was a moral issue. The complex which he felt in relation to Gustave Moreau was nothing less than a father complex. Without even realizing it, Rouault suppressed certain aspirations and repressed, or at least sublimated, in the Freudian sense of the word, his creative instincts. Once his master was no longer there, the constraints imposed upon him became more remonte. Pure idealism gave place to the search for the human document and the study of the facts, to the empirical spirit of observation and investigation.

Was Rouault to become the apologist of ugliness, as the Romantics were deemed to be? In discovering Paris, its human zoo, its factitious paradies, its ambiguous pleasures and its forbidden games, he displays all its flaws. The question, however, is not why, after painting the holy women, he turned to painting prostitutes, but rather *how* he painted them. This eye-witness who goes to the root of the matter is master of his techniques. His content and his form are one and the same. Although none of his works is a snapshot or a slice of life, he uses a form of shorthand. The *Chahut* (or Tabarin) (1904), that dance which Georges Seurat had immortalized, fixes the successive stages of a movement and records its internal mechanism. Rouault's kinetic drawing lends itself perfectly to this operation. The line is made up of a multitude of strokes. This line, with its intense power, remains extensible.

He dissociates colour from the volume which serves to support it. His tones act of their own volition. *Tabarin* is a harmony of blues, set off by a few coral strands and emphasized by some reserves of white.

Water-colour on paper, then transferred to canvas, was the medium which best

Prostitute before a mirror (No. 2)
Watercolour and pastel

Private collection

met his desire of expression. Did he use it until the mid-1920's to the exclusion of all other techniques? This is not certain. His chemistry is more complex. He paints in ink and oil; gouache, Indian ink and coloured inks; pastel and oil; greasepaint, ink and oil; oil on paper; oil on canvas; oil and gouache on an engraved ground, and so forth.

Rouault's prostitutes display their charms and go through their paces before the customers in the brothels, those dismal cesspools of iniquity. Here is the sinister procession, pitiable but grandiose in its ignominy, of the hetairae bleached in harness, beasts of burden reduced to slavery from the age of puberty.

Are the *Fallen Eve* (1905) and the *Prostitute before a Mirror* (1906) deliberately sadistic paraphrases of the *Rokeby Venus* in the London National Gallery, which is probably the first modern nude of ancient painting? Rouault transforms liabilities into assets. For all her perversity and degradation, less real than apparent, the *Prostitute before a Mirror*, like Velazquez's presumed model, incarnates the eternal feminine.

Singly or in groups, Rouault's barrackroom Aphrodites represent the capital sins. They scandalized, though they bear no traces of eroticism or licence. Their faces are muzzles. Their swollen eyes are dead. Their flesh is flabby. Their bellies are bloated. Their sterile breasts hang like empty pouches. Their moist skin, ruined by paint, is furrowed with wrinkles. These living corpses, drenched in alcohol, are incapable of inspiring any physical desire. These priestesses of venal love are a *Memento Mori*.

Willingly or unwillingly, Rouault makes them pathetic symbols or mysterious archetypal images. One of his *Odalisques* (of 1907) is a *Maja Desnuda*. The charm which emanates from this divinity, or rather idol, and its morbid quality, freeze the blood in the veins. If her hideousness subjugates, dazzles and casts a spell, it is because the profound, sonorous and grave colouring is a source of enchantment.

Does contour escape Rouault as it escaped Cézanne? This contour which he stresses remains moving. It expresses the density of masses and renders superfluous any trompe-l'œil modelling.

The prostitutes of the licenced houses, those prisons without bars, those temples of debauchery, those charnel-houses are contrasted with studies which disclose a concern of a pre-eminently plastic nature. The artist measures and orchestrates his forms, which are linear and chromatic phrases. He seeks the rhymes or relationships of curves. He seems to forget his teratology or to exorcize his monsters...

Rouault's clowns try in vain to make us laugh. "I saw quite clearly", writes the painter "that the clown was myself, that it was us, nearly all of us". The show can start. The artist's countenance appears at regular intervals. If the *Wrestler*, that debonnaire colossus (1905), is brother to Daumier's mountebanks, the *Clown with a Drum* of 1903 is son to nobody! Rouault, who models by flat tints, constructs by colour and lays on his tones, which are square touches. His treatment (if not his materials) is what it

The cavalcade (1910)
Coloured lithograph

Private collection

G. Rouault 19

will be to the end of his life. It is a skilful mosaic treatment, which reminds one of the works composed of little cubes of stone, glass or even enamel in the churches of Torcello, Venice and Ravenna.

A superficial observer, relying on deceptive appearances, might hint that, in his clowns with their outrageously raddled faces, Rouault is mocking the sacred image of man, God's creature. Nothing of the sort. Slashed with pigmentary colours, scarred both with pencil strokes and brush strokes, if not with a palette knife, ravaged by the years, by fatigue and by disease, this image, this gaping wound, is always charged with humanity. It joins hands — why hide the fact? — with the image of Christ dying on the Cross, insulted and reviled by a raving mob.

Daumier's *Crispin and Scapin*, a canvas whose construction cannot fail to suggest certain similarities with another *Circus Parade* (1906), does not yield the key. Rouault, although he pays little attention to the researches of the Cubists, explodes form and only leaves the scattered fragments. His volumes overlap. They are disaggregated. The painter proceeds by juxtaposition and over-printing. But his ventures into formal surgery and vivisection have nothing theoretical or experimental about them. Even his least orthodox initiatives preserve the spontaneity of improvisations. That is not all. In some circus scenes, or rather fairground scenes, such as the *Wedding of Nini Patte-en-l'Air* (1905), Rouault foreshadows the raw art which was only to be defined a half-century later. He clears the decks of his gay learning. "The art of the fairground booths, that art of illiterates and its idiot images" (Rimbaud), nourishes his visual memory. After borrowing his data from them he succeeds in heightening their style.

At the same time, the same man was painting a picture of the Law Courts. In *The Convict* (1907), *The Judges* (1908) and *The Tribunal* (before 1910), the accused and those who are to judge them, bear the stamp of the same infamy. They are beasts in human form. All thought is absent from these heads, carved out with a sickle.

The Tribunal with its red-robed judges is one of Rouault's most powerful works. Apart from perspective and format, this lugubrious assembly of puppets cannot fail to remind us of Goya's *Junta of the Philippines*.

Rouault's leitmotifs, in addition to judges and prostitutes, pierrots, dancers, clowns and pantaloons, are all the humiliated and the bruised, the crucified Christ, town and country landscapes, mystic or legendary landscapes and bathers, all of whose elements merge in an effect of general harmony, skeletons and flowers, horses and portraits, real or imaginary; the self-portraits, the portraits of Madame Baignères with her son, of Vollard, of André Suarès, of Bloy, Huysmans, Verlaine...

The painter of the *Aunt Sallys* (1907), waiting to be shot down, one by one, is the same as the painter of the *Fountains of Versailles* (1907), an animated landscape drawn in a shorthand of unusual boldness, and *the Bridge*, that off-centre picture whose asymmetry surprises at first sight, but which reveals a spirit of invention worthy of the masters of baroque painting, Tintoretto, El Greco, Tiepolo...

Clown with inkpot (1905)   Pastel, gouache and Indian ink
Private collection

Silhouette of woman
with little dog
1908
Ink, watercolour and pastel

Private collection

Woman
with feathered hat
1909
Ink and watercolour

Private collection

The Route of a great Artist

About 1910, Rouault makes a fresh start. If it is so difficult to detect the sources of his inspiration it is because his relations with the history of art are not those of Ingres with the Primitives and Raphael, of Eugène Delacroix with Rubens, of Manet with Hals and Velazquez or of Renoir with Delacroix and Fragonard. The painters mentioned knowingly exposed themselves to certain influences and later absorbed them. In Rouault's case, the analogies with Christian art of the first centuries, early Christian art and Roman-Byzantine art, can be explained only because the same causes produce the same effects. Art ceases to be a means of representation, the measure of which is set by the human body. By the visible it suggests the invisible. This transition from one state to another was to be heavy with consequence. The drawing becomes stiffer. In appearance, the proportions change. In reality, they are rediscovered. A broad black line encloses the volume like a lead frame. The line followed by Rouault is not a regression. It is a new birth.

The ardour of Cézanne, who, in his youth, accepted the perilous lesson of Caravaggio gradually gives place to a more static art. The portraits of Madame Paul Cézanne have the rhythm and the straight perpendiculars of mediaeval sculpture. The canons of Rouault's characters are those of Roman pediments, where the figures bend to the law of the setting.

In drawing and then engraving on stone the *Men and Horses* (1910), is Rouault departing from this line? Is he invalidating this manner of vision? His form is tauter than it used to be. It is more vigorous. It conveys a feeling of effort. It is more strictly defined. Seen in profile, Rouault's stallions are derived from the coursers sculptured by Donatello and Andrea Verrocchio, by Bernini, Coysevox, the Coustous and Falconet... They recall the *Free Horses* painted by Géricault. They have their bone structure, their muscular system and their nervous system, their energy and their vital impulse. The artist was later to paint circus equestriennes and two pictures of Joan of Arc on horseback of a hieratic splendour.

As he matured, Rouault withdrew into himself. His landscapes are no longer things seen, open-air visions observed and painted from the subject. They are perceived in the mind's

28

eye. These eloquent landscapes form the theatre for a mute but expressive dramatic action. Their light is the light of a lunar night.

A Parisian of Parisians, Georges Rouault is the product of an eminently urban civilization. He looks on nature like a townsman. Though he maintained contacts with Brittany, his ancestral country on the father's side, and with the Ile-de-France, where he was born, his elected homeland is the city. His skies are low. His leafless trees are as sad as gibbets or as melancoholy as factory chimneys.

Desolate landscapes of the inner or outher suburbs. Travellers without luggage, old men and women, flee in the dusk. Rouault has foreshadowed the exodus of the two wars. Peasants torn from the soil, Jews driven from their homes, signpost his endless roads.

Landscapes of winter or scorched earth... The sordid *Houses of the Poor* shake on their foundations. They are covered with leprosy. Christ visits the industrial zone *(Christ in the suburbs*, 1920). Children crowd round him. Christ mingles with men. He is at one with them. Rouault, who sees him, who exalts his presence and who lives the Gospel, is the painter of a new Christianity and of the Church of the poor.

Rouault gradually drops his sardonic accent. If he still savages the judiciary *(Three Judges*, 1924) he maltreats them in a different manner. His square-headed judges have nothing human about them. They remain blind and deaf. They know no pity. But it is a pleasure to see in these studies men, with rough-hewn torsos and obtuse visages, not marionettes or anthropoids, but personified powers of evil.

Rouault gives a moral nobility to his circus folk and mountebanks. From the particular, he goes to the general. Whether he paints the *Pierrot in profile* (1925) or the *Old Clown with a dog* (1925), he is seeking that quasi-monolithic style which will henceforth prevail in his work. For round-hand he substitutes an angular drawing. His form is rough-hewn. Its schematicism and its geometrism are those of thirteenth-century stonework. The tendency to enclose planes is that of the glass-workers of Chartres and Rheims. So is the flamboyant colouring.

The Couple
(M. and Mme. Poulot)
1905
Watercolour and gouache

Private collection

In 1932 Rouault painted the *Wounded Clown* and the *Little Family*, pictures surrounded by rich ornamental borders. Each of these strictly enclosed compositions has three figures. They came after the great *Nude* with intersecting planes (1925) and the *Pierrot* with the polyhedral head (1925), and before the *Old King* (1937). A harmony in malachite and amber, jade and sapphire, porphyry and tortoiseshell, the *Old King* betrays its affiliation. It is a dazzling tribute to Delacroix, with the features and the gold-embroidered robe of Sardanapalus, dying on the pyre raised in his palace, surrounded by his treasures, his women and his eunuchs.

Rouault multiplies his disturbing images of young girls with sinuous smiles. During the nineteen-thirties we find these enigmatic masks with their dilated irises, recalling the Palmyra steles, the coinage of the Later Roman Empire and the funerary portraits of Fayum. Rouault is haunted by the Orient of the spirit; *Veronica* (1945), *The Sibyl of Cumae* (1947), *Theresina* (1947).

Many historians maintain that after the age of seventy he loses his ancient fury and that his work is no longer animated by sacred ire. Has the discovery of the inner life calmed him? Has he found the path to serenity? This bright interval, or at least this lessening of tension, is no doubt only an empty word. The spectacle is that of the blossoming of a personality about to attain its culminating point. Like Cézanne, Renoir and Bonnard, but also like the great masters of previous centuries, Titian and Rembrandt, Rouault achieves the transmutation of his raw material. This miracle worker merges painting and prayer, prayer and poetry. His treatment thickens. It becomes clotted. Chrome yellows predominate in the painter's register alongside the carmines and Veronese greens. Fantastic flowers make their appearance.

Rouault's colour is a fired terra-cotta. It does not adhere to the form, but engenders form by a detour. It assumes such relief that it becomes perceptible to the touch. The graphic scaffolding fades away. A magma of pigments takes its place. The motif emerges from this fusion of adhesive tones brutally projected onto the canvas or laid on with a trowel.

Only Rembrandt in his later works went so far in a direction which renounces all illusionism and before which one can speak as much of *tachisme* as of informal style. But yet Rembrandt is not, any more than Rouault, a dreamer dabbling in ashes. This magician, or rather this alchemist, is a craftsman moulding his substance of colours with the inner intention of calling forth from it a world of images and of countenances which invite contemplation.

Sarah (1956) and *Theodora* (1956) are sister-works of Rembrandt cleansed of their centuries of deposit and their thick coat of bronze varnish.

But this accent, or vertiginous rise to the light, is neither an ode to reconquered life nor a chant of joy. A solar painter, Rouault intones a hymn to God and proclaims the final victory of celestial light. His fortune is so vast that it cannot be figured; it extends to limitless space.

The Sense of the Divine

If Rouault's work is one of the great chapters of painting it is because, while linked to its own age by certain conventions, it transcends the passing moment. This work dominates its century. It reflects the permanence of man and expresses it in its very depth. The influence of the time does not explain Rouault's genius, since in art and philosophy there is no progress. Michelangelo does not dethrone Verrocchio any more than Aristotle dethrones Plato.

Rouault is a Christian painter not because he deals with themes of biblical inspiration, but because he brings, even to his secular work, the sense of the marvellous and of the supernatural.

"God is dead," proclaimed Nietzsche. But he immediately asked "How can we fill this terrible void?" Is his cry of distress a sacrilege or the *credo* of an atheist? Be that as it may, God is born again in the work of Rouault. This God is not a mere mental acceptance. His reality is forced upon our minds. "It is not God who is a myth. It is the myths which reveal the Divine Presence in the human soul." (Jung.)

Rouault's religious pictures, his landscapes and his compositions, are not diaphanous and impalpable works. They conserve their physical properties. Their organic matter is vibrant. But what is this matter which the artist transfigures, if not the bread of life and a source of creative energy?

The earliest works of a sacred character which Rouault painted after the crucial year (or crucial years) of his metamorphosis are a *Crucifixion* (1913), several *Holy Faces* (1913) and a *Baptism of Christ* (1913). Other *Holy Faces* signpost the work of the painter. The most poignant are those of 1933 and 1945. The expression in their inordinately large eyes seems to be fluid, enchanting and undermining all nervous resistance. Their charm is hypnotic. Their power remains occult.

Rouault's *Holy Faces* are duplicates. Some of them have the wild beauty of Coptic portraits. Death lays a mask over these living faces. "For death is an absolute mask" (Bachelard).

Rouault's Christ is not a Jupiter Tonans or the Pantocrator of the dazzling Byzantine basilicas. He is a Christ who has shed his blood and suffered for all of us. The scenes of his Passion are set above eye level, or at ground level. Christ is alone or flanked by apostles or holy women. Rouault does not confine himself to presenting objectively the impious punishment of the crucifixion. Like the old Gothic painters, he revives all the bitterness of the sufferings endured by the Redeemer. He feels those sufferings himself. He associates us with them and communicates them to us...

Rouault's art is not, and never was, a problem which is posed and solved. It is a mystical and poetic datum which intuition enables us to grasp. Thus, Rouault is the creator of the only religious landscapes which can have been painted, drawn or engraved since those of Rembrandt. Some of them are set in the Paris suburbs or the north of France. There man is ground down by a hostile and malevolent environment. No plant borders the empty highway. Omnipresent, the powers of darkness, machinery and legalized poverty lord it over the mining country. Advanced industrial society has reared here "dark satanic mills" which are casemates, storehouses, garages, mining villages and sheds polluted by smoke. Is the Christ who communes with himself in this mournful setting of sprawling towns a worker-priest? Indeed not. If he makes the gesture of benediction and gathers to him all the outcast of the earth, he does not adopt their dress and bearing. The Son of Man lives outside time and space.

The fabulous landscapes of the Holy Land are much more propitious to meditation and more enchanting. Beneath an ember sky, the Saviour is outlined against a ground of palm groves, sand dunes and buildings which are, or could be, mosques with their minarets.

The landscapes of the Lake of Tiberias, where Christ performed a miracle, those landscapes which Rouault never saw, although he gives them every warrant of credibility, are the high places of the Christian West. The artist represents them without regard to terrestrial contingencies. Everything has again become what it was at the birth or in the childhood of the world *(The Lake of Tiberias,* 1950). Rouault shows us the *Christ Reviled* (1932, 1939, 1942...), *Christ before his judges* and *Christ in the house of Martha and Mary* (or in the cell of some chain-gang convict) (1950). He sanctifies everything he touches and all those who approach him.

We do not know the iconography of Rouault's Christ. It slips through the net of exegesis. Rouault has his own vanity. He refuses to imitate the manner of the ancients. If he creates or re-creates his images, he identifies them with the ardent soul of his divine model. But he does not seek to innovate.

If Rouault asserts himself as an initiator and as a forerunner, Christ defies the test of time. He is the one who is forever.

The Court (1908)
Watercolour and gouache

Private collection

The Drunkard
1905
Watercolour and pastel

Musée d'Art Moderne
City of Paris

Nude (about 1917)
Indian ink wash

Private collection

Rouault and the printed Book

The books written and illustrated, or merely illustrated, by Rouault are one of the glories of French publishing. Pride of place must be given to *Miserere*, published by Éditions de l'Étoile Filante in autumn, 1947, but conceived during the Great War, some thirty years earlier. This monumental work consists of 58 plates (format 63 × 53 cm). The text is by Rouault. The technique of the prints alternates between engraving, aquatint and etching, etc.

Les réincarnations d'Ubu appeared in 1932, published by Éditions Vollard. The book consists of 21 original etchings and 109 drawings by Rouault engraved on wood by Auber. *Le Cirque de l'Étoile Filante* dates from 1936. The text by Rouault is enriched with etchings and numerous drawings (Éditions Ambroise Vollard). *Passion* came off the press in 1939. The text is by André Suarès. Rouault illustrated it with original colour etchings and wood engravings (Éditions Ambroise Vollard). Baudelaire's *Les Fleurs du Mal* with 14 plates engraved by Rouault appeared in 1966 (Éditions de l'Étoile Filante).

In engraving *Miserere*, which is his master-work, Rouault composed his testament, a living synthesis of his vision. His texts are lapidary; they are parables. They may seem to be uneven, but nevertheless make up a uniform whole with a profound inner unity.

Miserere may be regarded as a parallel between the Calvary of Christ and the martyrdom of the innocent who die tortured and reviled. This lamentation is an act of faith. Its last plate

is a luminous *Holy Face* bearing this inscription in Rouault's writing *"C'est par ses meurtrissures que nous sommes guéris"* — by his wounds are we healed.

Miserere, whose black and white contrasts create a rhythm of aerial values of aggressive power, is a work of drama. The Stations of the Cross on this *via dolorosa* are the artist's usual themes: *Jesus reviled... and scourged*, the ragged ones, *Tatterdemalions of misfortune*, the mad king, the painter in the guise of a clown, his face averted, the landscapes, the *Suburbs of long-suffering*, the *Ladies of "Pleasure"*, the so-called women of the town, the stricken cities, the Virgins with Child (or Motherhoods), and the entombments, but also the grimacing simulacra of the new Teutonic Knights with the sub-titles, *Far from the smile of Rheims*, and *The more noble the heart, the less stiff is the neck.*

Dead men, arise! — "Debout les morts!" — The behind-the-lines heroes of the 1914 War always remember this high feat of arms related both by the war artists and the correspondents of the right-minded press of the day. Rouault's version naturally differs from that of a George Scott! The artist cries anathema on keen light-hearted war and the atrocious death of others, glorified in dithyrambic terms by the armchair strategists of the Jockey Club or the Army and Navy Club and the distinguished retired generals of the *Écho de Paris*. His skeletons rising up to the assault spring from a trench which is a communal grave and a sombre charnel-house. They inspire fear rather than admiration.

Had Rouault read *l'Enfer, le Feu, Au Dessus de la Mêlée, All Quiet on the Western Front* and *Quatre de l'Infanterie?* He hated war as a fraud. The figure of Death, in one of his prints, says to the little soldier, "It will be the last, old man", the famous war to end wars, that sanguinary myth which made men march and die to save their children's lives.

Vollard could have asked Rouault to illustrate Jarry's masterpiece. Instead, he invited his cooperation with his own variant of *Ubu Roi*. *Les Réincarnations d'Ubu*, of which Renoir's model, painted as a toreador, was proud to be the author, has the following chapters: *Colonial policy, Colonial problems and the League of Nations, Père Ubu in the Health Service, Père Ubu and flying, Père Ubu at the Post Office, Père Ubu in the Land of the Soviets.*

Vollard has neither Jarry's humour nor his satanic talent! His mockeries are threadbare and his sneers strike a false note. No matter! At grips with Ubu, Rouault tackles this scion of Panurge and Maître Pathelin. He delineates him in droll portraits, which are so many carnival masks or swollen heads. Ubu's colonial victims are negroes. They are stark naked, but they wear top hats. These black Africans, snatched from the barbarism of a tribal way of life, enjoy all the benefits of a civilization which the traders have imported from Europe; military service, forced labour, alcoholism and syphilis.

Prostitutes (1903)   Gouache and oil
Private collection

Exodus
Wash

Georges Rouault studio

The Health Service consists of former veterinary surgeons or even former butchers! At the front, a general who has just been appointed Grand Officer of the Legion of Honour celebrates his promotion by launching a thundering attack against the enemy's advanced posts.

Rouault, however thankless his task might appear, is quite at ease in standing against the wall and branding this brilliant company, in which the scoundrel rubs shoulders with the impostor and the trickster mingles with the myrmidon of the law.

Le Cirque de l'Étoile Filante has a text by Rouault, in which prose is mingled with verse. The artist devoted to the universe of the circus these pages with their admirable vocabulary, in turn studied and borrowed either from current speech or from the popular songs of the day or from an immemorial *Beggars' Opera*. We are reminded of Ferdinand Céline and Bertolt Brecht.

Rouault hails as "Knight of the sorrowful bones", or "daughter of the air", the acrobat or the tightrope dancer who defies the laws of equilibrium. His clowns with their livid faces and boneless bodies adore Christ, the king whose kingdom is not of this world.

Passion is the most prophetic text which Suarès has left to the world. Rouault's etchings, which are the visual comment on it, mark the advent of a new Christian art. After Rouault had rendered his soul to God, this art came to a sudden end despite the efforts of the most gifted artists of their generation to give it a new impetus. Vence, Assy, Ronchamp and Audincourt are exceptions which prove the rule.

Les Fleurs du Mal is a posthumous work, which Rouault had been preparing for a long time and for which he supervised the printing of the plates. These plates are a general illustration of Baudelaire's poems and reconstitute, by means of analogies, the state of mind of the author of *Spleen et Idéal*. Rouault brings out the sense of sin of a reprobate poet. Some of his engravings represent skeletons comparable with those of James Ensor. But the skeletons of the augur of Ostend are more witty and more diverting. These puppets and these scarecrows mingle in a kermesse or a masquerade which turns into a saturnalia. They deck themselves out with false noses, they dance a jig or play billiards, dress up in their cast-off clothing and wear feathered hats.

In his visions of the "blind Fury with the abhorred shears" Rouault measures up to Ligier Richier. His skeletons show their teeth, stare at us with cavernous eyes and rattle their bones. The skeletons of *Miserere* are no less terrible, no less ghostly than those of *Les Fleurs du Mal*. Baudelaire would have liked these death's-heads, who advance and palaver like Death following the knight in Dürer's print. Some of them whisper the words which, according to Genesis, God said to Adam after the original sin; "Dust thou art and unto dust thou shalt return".

Rouault is a genius marked by the Old Testament.

The Presence of Rouault

The optic from which Rouault's art must be looked at is that of the epoch, of which we are impassioned witnesses. Now, no epoch has challenged easel painting so vigorously. Even the validity of the Museums which Malraux, a few years ago, described as the new cathedrals, is called in question. All the ways of hanging, presenting and arranging the paintings of the old masters in public galleries now seem outdated and obsolete. We are witnessing a radical cultural revolution.

Should we burn down the Louvre, following the slogan which the Futurists, guided by Marinetti, claim to have invented, or should we smash its too rigid framework? Is not the Museum, that accumulation or sum of works of art of all times and all countries, that place of pilgrimage and meditation, nothing but an immense necropolis reserved for a minority of enlightened art-lovers, and a passive mass of visitors, whose leisure is organized by the State, the travel agencies and the tour organizers, with the declaration that they are entitled to culture? Art descends into the arena! Its mission is to integrate itself in collective and individual daily life and to humanize the great urban concentrations. That will be the price of its salvation.

This is not the first time that modern artists have tried to link their fate to town planning and architecture, to craftsmanship, to the theatre and to books. The Nabis, and Lautrec before them, design posters. They decorate screens. They are illustrators. At the beginning of their activity, their preferred field is murals. Maurice Denis decorates churches, museums and places of entertain-

The Baptism of Christ (No. 2), 1911   Ink, gouache and pastel
Private collection

ment. Maillol initiates himself to the trade of a tapestry weaver. To dye his wools he uses vegetable colours extracted from plants which he picks on the hillside. Roussel paints theatre curtains. Bonnard and Édouard Vuillard embellish the private houses of their collectors.

Rouault painted only one stage set, for the *Prodigal Son*, a ballet put on by Diaghilev the very year of his death, in 1929. He had no walls available. Both at Assy and other sanctuaries he executed only a few stained-glass windows, those gems which enflame the atmosphere around them. But the spirit in which he treats most of his work, paintings, drawings, prints, which date from his maturity, is not that of chamber painting in the strict classical sense of the term. His figures and his heads are not on the scale of the plane surfaces in which they are inscribed. Amplified and treated in close-up, they adhere to an invisible wall. They operate as shock values and produce a veritable impact. Their construction is deliberately reduced to the essential and simplified, as it is in the frescoes of the twelfth century.

A home for all men. The cathedral was a Gospel in stone, which men could read without knowing the alphabet. Rouault's images, images which are parables, play a similar role and fill a similar function. They are addressed to man, seen as a whole and in his plenitude. They prove that the artist rejects both the scholastic conventions and the ciphered idiom of the new *avant-garde* of art. He opens a dialogue. His work requires and implies no gloss. In contrast, when his monumental style engravings, those of the *Miserere*, bear a few lines of text, the narrative element and the plastic element are closely and intimately united. Each of these plates can be likened to a wall newspaper.

Rouault breaks down the staunch barriers arbitrarily erected between flat painting and every other form of visual art.

His art is a global and integral language. Anchored in the divine, the master of the *Railwayman* and *Christ among the doctors* has no herd instinct. He resists the power of the world and preserves his personality intact. His work is a whole. It is indivisible. It is complete, just as Rouault is a complete artist; painter, draughtsman, engraver, enamel worker and stained glass worker, mime, reciter, tragedian, comedian and demiurge.

Like Erasmus, Rouault the sage sings the praises of folly; "I have been so happy painting, a painting fool, forgetting everything in the blackest gloom."

Nude (1917)
Indian ink wash

Private collection

Landscape, with blue distance (about 1910)
Crayon and oil-paint thinned with turpentine

Private collection

The Hovel (about 1913)

Gouache, ink, distemper and pencil

Musée d'Art Moderne, City of Paris

II

Georges Rouault, my Father

"Childhood Memories are graven on my Heart"

In the Rue de l'École de Médicine in Paris in 1885 you could learn to draw in the evening classes at the School of Decorative Arts. The janitors often used to see a young boy running up, out of breath, frightened of being late and of finding the doors shut. He used to come on foot from the Barrière de Clichy, right on the other side of Paris, after his day's work as an apprentice stained glass maker. The first evening, his neighbour, Bussy, asked him in a whisper "What is your name?" "Georges Rouault". "How old are you?" "Fourteen".

My father was born during the Commune, on 27 May, 1871; while Paris was still burning; he often used to tell the story of his birth:

"No one wanted to take my mother down to the cellar to shelter from the shelling." A shell had gone through the room at 51 Rue de la Villette, where the young woman had sought refuge with her father. "My grandmother had gone off to fetch a doctor, but she could not find anybody, doctor or midwife. They called out to her, "Citizen!... help me to bury the dead, take a paving stone". The poor woman, whose shoulder was out of joint, could hardly lift it."

Versailles
(The fountain)
1905

Private
collection

The Flood (1910)
Watercolour

Private collection

Meanwhile, "Jeanne, a little servant girl with a heart of gold, in spite of 'having her blood curdled', saved both mother and child"... by taking the young woman down to the cellar, where, at half past twelve in the afternoon, she gave birth to a boy, Georges Henry. He was baptized on 25 June "at Saint-Leu, said to be the parish of Villon".

Belleville was a village, and the child soon became familiar with every inch of its streets, which he was afterwards to transpose into the tragic mode in the *Faubourgs des Longues Peines*.

"If you are a good little boy, my pet, we will go to the Rue des Solitaires and watch them light the lamps", Modeste Delphine would say, the second wife of Alexandre Champdavoine, Georges' maternal grandfather. She loved her step-daughter Louise, my grandmother, as much as she loved her own daughters, Henriette and Marie. These "little aunts", bohemian and very gay, used to paint porcelain vases. They thought it wiser, one fine day, to turn civil servants. Not enamoured of Louise's marriage with a craftsman, Alexandre Rouault, they would respond to the teasing of Georges, who 'to vex them' would flaunt a workman's blue shirt. They adored the child and they therefore encouraged their elder sister to set aside as they did 20 francs out of their monthly 83 francs, to help their nephew; and all this with a joyful heart. It was a house where you could not help always being in fits of laughter.

"I am sure my mother had very great gifts. People used to say she had the bump of mathematics. And yet my grandfather decided she should be a dressmaker, like her mother; it was very odd for such an intelligent man... and so my mother set about her dressmaking... One of my aunts met her one day with a parcel a yard high on her shoulder... It was some dresses which the seamstresses had not delivered in time, and my mother had sat up all night putting the finishing touches to them. And so she was very happy to find a permanent job with the Savings Bank in the Rue St Romain. My aunts were rather ashamed of being employed by the Post Office, but she was delighted to leave her office at six, her day's work done; 'It is the best day of my life, she would say...'

"She used to get up at dawn to do terrible calculations which then had to be checked from fifty-page notebooks which she used to bring home as extra work." Later on, the teacher at the College of Fine Arts was to ask his favourite pupil about his family. "Gustave Moreau wanted to meet her. He was astonished that, unlike Madame X. she did not say 'My son is a genius.' 'Does she realise what you have done?' he added, 'your *Child Jesus?*'

"When he learned that my mother used to get up at dawn to do extra work to help me, his impulse dried up all at once and he was even very moved:

> Your mother has grown old
> That you may paint,
> Young in heart and spirit,
> For all her toil and travail,
> A veteran of life's war."

Alexandre Rouault, one of a large family in Montfort (in Ille-et-Vilaine) was a piano varnisher. "My father toured the whole of France on foot. In the old days you used to go and see how people worked elsewhere. He used to waken me every morning by putting a damp towel over my eyes, declaiming 'Brutus, thou sleep'st. Awake!'

"Like a sensible man, he was afraid of my being a painter, enormously afraid of it. He would have liked me to take up a solid trade. It was not that my father wished me ill. But you must remember how people regarded painters at that time; they were looked upon as a sort of poisonous fungus. Nowadays it is just the opposite. My father did not behave badly at all, he behaved like a good father...

"... One day when Moreau saw my father arriving with my two big canvases on a handcart with me pushing behind, he was shocked. I said to him 'It is quite natural, Sir, we are people who are accustomed to manual labour.' 'You should have told me' replied Moreau, 'I would have sent to fetch them.' He was shocked to see the poor man panting and me behind pushing the barrow."

Georges had an elder sister, Émilie, who married Arthur Thomas; their son André became a decorator in Algiers. A travelling circus would sometimes climb the hill to Belleville; at an early age, Georges was impressed by the images of clowns, bareback riders and acrobats. The family took no holidays; excursions into the woods at Meudon had to suffice. They read, they copied out books; at family meals they sang: "There was a religious silence when, under family pressure I recited *Bara, the heroic drummer-boy* on the dark staircase. If I repeated the lines of Shakespeare's King Lear I felt transported into another world... I remember, in my grandfather's house in the Rue de Sévigné there were busts of Racine, Molière and Voltaire above my head... Brought face to face with reality as a child, I belonged to the school of Daumier before I got to know Raphael..."

Alexandre Champdavoine had copied out *Orlando Furioso* in his own hand; he read Gœthe and Spinoza, collected reproductions of Rembrandt, Manet, Daumier. On seeing his four-year-old grandson drawing on the kitchen flagstones he very happily recognized his gifts. With his son-in-law, he was an admirer of Lamennais and Victor Hugo, to whose funeral he took the child Georges, riding on his shoulders. At the infant school, the boy was advised to continue his studies, he was so brilliant. In the school in the Rue des Poissonniers, and later in the Rue des Fourneaux, he walked off with nearly all the prizes. On the fly-leaf of *Don Quixote,* his school prize, he wrote "I have read this admirable book again and again, and grown to like it more and more so that, in pictorial art I am willing to be called Quixotic."

By constant raps over the knuckles one schoolmaster had awakened the interest of this good pupil. Another took him on a two day trip to Le Havre, Rouen and Honfleur. The harassing

Landscape (the Barge), about 1910–12
Distemper and pastel

Musée d'Art Moderne, City of Paris

excursion ended with a hot bath at Saint-Lazare Station in Paris, "which finished us off", said my father, "but as there was still some money left that scrupulously honest man gave us all savings books." This modest sum helped Rouault to enrol at the College of Fine Arts.

Georges lost his grandfather the year of his fourteenth birthday. From that day until his own death he always wore a portrait medallion of him. The same year he began his apprenticeship with Tamoni. "Tamoni was rather a hard master", we were told by René Bour, the friend who went with Georges to draw lots for conscription and with whom he never lost touch. That day Georges, like other lads born in the "terrible year", was rejected on medical grounds, and, after many check-ups, remained unfit for military service; all his life he was subject to paroxysms of tachycardia.

"When we fired our glass there was a whole pile of pieces heaped up on a tray, which had to be lifted; I could do it, but Georges was not very strong. He must have suffered more than I did, he was younger. He was far from good-tempered; Herman, the clerk, thought he could tame this young apprentice a bit. Far from it. Sometimes there were rows, but Georges always stood up to him. He had boundless energy and a fire which I lacked. Tamoni used to say 'Go to such and such a place in the Rue Popincourt to fetch this or that. Here are eight sous for the omnibus there and back.' Georges would set off at a brisk pace and trot as far as the Rue Popincourt. He came back at the same pace and pocketed the eight sous to buy paints; I thought that was marvellous, he amazed me."

In the streets Georges was "a bit unsociable" — "Here comes So-and-so, let's make ourselves scarce."

It wasn't that he was unfriendly, but with his comrades, in general, he did not want to waste a moment of his time.

"After my apprenticeship with Tamoni I scoured the whole of Paris for a week, looking for work. I had the list of stained glass makers; there weren't very many of them. I came home crestfallen one night and said to my mother, 'Listen, I don't know what we're going to do, I haven't found anything.' There was only Papa Hirsch left. He welcomed me like a father, like a saviour, and he cried when I left in 1892."

Georges did the drawings and assembled the cames and earned fifty centimes a week.

"If there had been fine stained glass as there used to be in the Middle Ages, perhaps I should never have become a painter... but it was commercial glasswork. The craftsman side of the work had been dropped, the side of the man who loves the material he is working with..."

In the evenings he went to the School of Decorative Art and got up at dawn to draw — at an easel his father had made him — before leaving for work.

"We had moved to 204 Boulevard St Germain, so that my father could be near his work. I was very happy at this, that was where I did all my studying... the only room I had was a little corridor, the size of a couple of cupboards... To get a little peace and quiet, I fitted a bolt. It was in that corridor that I painted canvases as big as the *Child Jesus* (120 cm. long). I had to sleep in that hallway for years. I used to put up a camp bed every night."

At Hirsch's he would sometimes handle fragments of old stained glass sent in for restoration; "Then I used to be in the seventh heaven... I dreamed of being the servitor of those beloved old masters, so remote from any commercialism, and I would shut my eyes and call up the image of them, distracted for an instant from the ridiculous work I was made to do, a parody of what I would have liked to do with flame-pure colours."

Successful in the competitive entrance examination for the College of Fine Arts, Rouault hesitated to give up his livelihood, but his drawings at the School of Decorative Arts had impressed a member of the Institut de France, who invited their author to do the stained glass work for the College of Pharmacy. This sign of confidence encouraged him to take his decision; on 3 December, 1890, he joined the College of Fine Arts. He was not yet twenty.

In spite of the harassing life, and the anxiety about the future, his vitality was enormous; in the evening he would stand upright at the foot of his parents' bed and jump down upon them from its full height, with loud shouts. Attracted by physical exercise, he was rarely able to indulge in it. He was thin and five foot six inches tall. "People said I looked like Alfred de Musset."

He did not always have the sixteen sous he needed to lunch in the Rue de la Huchette on "chips and cockroaches"; a family arrangement was made; his father's brother, a pharmacist, agreed — on certain terms — to take him in at midday. Uncle Charles had no faith in his nephew's future. He kept on saying so. His nephew, white with rage, answered him back roundly. But these pinpricks could not discourage a young man full of enthusiasm, who had just taken a decisive step.

After drawing in the "galleries" for two years and passing a great many examinations, he went to see Delaunay, his teacher. "I had a roll in my hands, a roll of drawings. I was with a friend at the foot of the great stone staircase. Delaunay looked... he gave them all back to me and then he said 'It's very good, very good,' and went on up the stairs. I can still see my friend, like the great buffoon he was (he spent his life joking), bursting into laughter. 'You idiot!' I said, 'what is there to laugh

Winter (about 1910)
Crayon and oil-paint thinned with turpentine

Private collection

The Acrobat (about 1913)
Watercolour and Indian ink

Musée d'Art Moderne,
City of Paris

about ?'...   I ran after old Delaunay at full speed, and just as he was turning the door-handle, I yelled in his ear 'I want to paint!.' The poor man was terrified; he looked at me for an instant with a dumbfounded air, and then said, 'Very well, very well, I will enroll you both.'

Delaunay died a few months later and was succeeded by Gustave Moreau. Rouault felt an immediate admiration for this very exceptional teacher, whose favourite pupil he became:

"He was strongly and covertly opposed, both in the College and elsewhere... I think what irritated people about him was that spiritual sense which he set up in opposition to natural- ism and a certain official conformism... What consideration he had, what a delicate respect for life and its subtleties! 'I hope that your success will be slow in coming,' he would say to me. 'An artist who has his own little house by the time he is thirty is finished for a certain art... I see you more and more isolated and solitary; you love a grave and sober, essentially religious, art...' "

The master sent the pupil to the Opera, to the theatre, gave him the run of his library. He wrote little notes to his "dear child" full of "affectionate friendship".

At the Studio, Rouault listened to him: "I was dumb, I answered Yes or No, that was all." Not always, however. "At the Studio," Paul Baignères told me, "you heard nobody but him." This cultivated, sensitive and intelligent friend encouraged my father with a remarkable wisdom and clarity of judgement.

Fifty years later, on the occasion of an exhibition, he wrote "While I was exam- ining your water-colours, I noticed a dark patch at my feet. On looking more closely I saw it was a dead butterfly lying on its back. I turned it over. What magic! That sober brown of the back exalted into a dull red, the wings surmounted by a yellow disc outlined in black and then in violet. It has been decorated by Rouault, I said to myself, it is the same daring. Rouault has arrived at the same result as the Creator. He has thus proved the truth of Shelley's fine words, that art is 'the visitations of the divinity in man.' "

Another friend, Léon Lehmann, was also shrewd enough to discern his excep- tional gifts from the very outset: "His pencil or pen drawings were taut, firm and elegant in their construc- tion... The atmosphere in the Studio was one of charming comradeship. Rouault was greatly loved, as much for his simple, cordial, sprightly character as for the pride and the lofty joys his talent aroused in us. The ardour he put into his work was prodigious... we looked upon him as a prince."

Lehmann, "dazzled and intimidated", never addressed a word to his comrade at the College. A sick man, he lived in the Provinces, and some years later met him by accident: "Rouault came straight up to me, asked why I had disappeared, and showed an interest in me which overwhelmed me with surprise and gratitude."

Christ reviled (1912)
Distemper and pastel

Private collection

The next day, my father came up to Lehmann again. "I have found you somewhere to live," he said, and took him home to his parents.

"Rouault's father and mother were admirable and I had the greatest veneration for them. Rouault, for his part, displayed an extraordinary delicacy: never did he try to influence me. I gradually recovered, thanks to this friend, whom the best of doctors could not have equalled."

"Outside the Louvre the sky is clear and the horizon is light. Young Matisse thoughtfully watches the two pale gold arms encircling the island of the Vert Galant... Moreau bids him speak his innermost thoughts. There is a certain amount of wrangling, in all frankness and friendship."

Matisse and Rouault, lifelong friends, squabbled joyfully every time they met: "For goodness sake! will you let me get a word in?" Matisse would shout.

Bonhomme, for his part, parodied Cézanne, and even his comrades.

Although his pupil had won the Prix Chenavard and the Prix Fortin d'Ivry, Moreau was vexed to see him deprived of the Prix de Rome: "... What are you doing in this gang?", he said. "Work at home."

Meanwhile, on visits to the Louvre, he had taught his pupils to love Rembrandt, Le Lorrain, Poussin, Corot, Giorgione, as well as "the frescoes of the Primitives, although his own research lay in another direction".

Rouault continued to submit his work to his "master" and brought him the first-fruits of his personal research, such as *Landscape by Night*. In 1898 this deeply venerated friend was carried off by cancer of the tongue. Moreau had made Georges promise never to smoke.

My old Master has left me.
To him I was never a novice or a pupil
But the happy confidant of his lively thought.

Small red and gold Page
(1941)
Gouache
for "Divertissement"

Private collection

The Universe of Rouault

Rouault was now to experience solitude; he had persuaded his parents and his aunts to go to Algiers, where he had a widowed sister with a child. They stayed there a year.

"If my art is harsh, it is no doubt owing to this period in my life."

He lived from hand to mouth, often not eating his fill.

The observation of life, "that infinite sadness of life" — street scenes, faces glimpsed in the Law Courts and sketched on returning home (to be worked over again and again in the coming years) — helped him to constitute his universe.

"Home" was sometimes a corner of a studio lent him by Georges Desvallières out of pity for his penury, sometimes hotel rooms; a little later, he rented a studio in the Rue de La Rochefoucault, where Renoir was his neighbour on the same landing. They did not know each other, for "I should never have dared to speak to him first."

In 1903, Rouault was appointed Curator of the Gustave Moreau Museum, with a modest salary, proper living quarters and the moral support of Henry Rupp, Moreau's friend, whose affection was touching and whose judgement was lucid: "When shall I see you working", he complained, "with a little serenity and even a little lightness of heart?"

In answer to a comment on the "bad temper" of his young friend, he replied, in his piping voice, "No! He has spirit and no one has more."

He spent a few months in the monastery at Ligugé and came back to Paris in October, 1901, with Huysmans, already very ill... He died of cancer after many months of suffering.

This agony profoundly affected my father, who had become attached to the writer and took his part with Léon Bloy, to whom he was introduced by Marguillier, secretary of the *Gazette des Beaux-Arts*.

Thanks to Father Vallée — a friend of his comrade Piot — my father had entered into communion with the Church some years before. He was overwhelmed by reading *La Femme Pauvre*

White Pierrot (1941)
Gouache
for "Divertissement"

Private collection

and wanted to meet the author. But Marguillier's role did not end there. For many years he provided support and counsel, introducing the painter to the review *Mercure de France*, and to his friends, receiving unexpected visits from him, as witnessed by the hundreds of letters written to him by Rouault, which his daughter Suzanne has very generously given us.

At this stage Coquiot, Marcel Sembat, Dr. Girardin, Druet, Monsieur and Madame Henri Simon bought pictures such as *The Barge, The Staircase,* and *Clown with Accordion.* Rouault was a member of the selection committee for the Salon d'Automne, where he himself exhibited, as he did at the Salon des Indépendants. In 1907, in an epic encounter, he defended Matisse's *La Coiffeuse* against a President who shouted "... I don't give a fig for the regulations!"

"I am beginning to get letters asking me to use my influence... and when will somebody exercise a little useful influence on my behalf? Sometimes I know how to ask favours for other people, but I am incapable of doing it for myself... I have got plenty to do between now and 27 September. If I am a man of iron, I shall manage it all before and then I shall take a complete rest... conclusion; I shall be a man of iron..."

This dream of a "complete rest" was hardly to be realized. He wanted to show: "Sixty little things which Desvallières can see and show round, twenty little pastels, very small clowns, five or six large ones and ten or so landscapes; all this may arouse great hostility." These last two words, underlined, are significant: they refer to his new line of research.

Meanwhile, the family circle had been re-formed; he dictated his mail to his mother, as he was to do for many years. I can still see my grandmother on the staircase, groaning, her head between her hands, and her vibrant son shouting in crescendo "Trumpet, trumpet!" (her ear-trumpet).

Marguillier used to get art books and reproductions. Rouault wanted Lehmann and Bignères to share in this pleasure:

"Thank you for welcoming my friends so charmingly... I am just finishing sending in to the Salon d'Automne and there will be an outcry, but I cannot help it, that is the road I want to take..." A perilous road, which he followed alone. Marguillier even spoke to him of "moral responsibility", but, as the sole witness of his friend's spiritual evolution, he knew how to preserve absolute discretion. My father asked him in 1904 to give Abbé Mugnier a letter which we have just been able to acquire through the hazards of the sale-room:

"I love my art passionately, and there is a growing conflict between my art and my religion... It is at the very moment when I have the greatest need of religion to sustain me in life and in art, that the advice and counsel of very religious and very respectable Catholics have filled me with some confusion... You can well understand what it is to be an artist... so dedicated to his work that it fills him with sadness to see that the conflict might end deplorably in letting go of religion..."

Marguillier remained the confidant:

"I believe in God and I also believe that he will help me to come through... I am succumbing under the weight of my sufferings and, perhaps, too, in all humility, under the weight of the sufferings of others... The Catholics have killed me... at a moment when I was seeking profound consolation. They have a horror of any *action*, as well as the certainty (and the mad pride inspired by that certainty) that they are in possession of the truth... They will be living more and more in a narrow circle, which will go on shrinking. If a man like Bloy were at the centre of it, holding *La Femme Pauvre* in one hand, and *Le Désespéré* in the other, it would be different..."

At the Salon d'Automne in 1905, Rouault showed *The Couple* (Monsieur and Madame Poulot), inspired by Bloy's characters. Bloy was furious: "He wanted to do my Poulots; I will not have such an illustration at any price..." *Tabarin*, the *Prostitute*, the *Aunt Sallys*, "with its ourageous lyricism", shocked him, but did he not see the highly poetic landscapes of this epoch?

"How often in the following years", writes Raïssa Maritain, "have we not seen Rouault at Bloy's place, standing up, with a distant look, his face apparently emotionless, but growing paler when the question of modern art was broached? Rouault grew pale and preserved a heroic silence. But always, in spite of this opposition on the whole question of his art, he remained faithful to Bloy... He went on working in the midst of the innumerable obstacles which poverty creates."

Bloy's conclusion was harsh: "You are exclusively attracted by ugliness." Rouault was to explain later: "If I have made the judges such lamentable figures, it was no doubt because I was translating the anguish I feel at the sight of a human being who is to judge other men... If I happen to have confused the judge's head with the head of the prisoner, this error reflects my own confusion."

In 1907, my father went with Baignières to Methey's, where for some years he had ceramics fired. The same year, in a letter to Marguillier, my mother's name appears for the first time: "If you get a letter or a call from Monsieur le Sidaner asking for information about me, don't be surprised... nothing happens, or will happen to me, I am convinced, except by the hand of providence..."

Baignères, on being approached, replied "My impressions are excellent; this young girl seems to have a very good understanding of the rare qualities of your nature. They do not leap to the eyes of those who are accustomed to the too facile spectacles of life."

Had not the good Gruyer said "No girl in good society would be willing to marry you, my poor Rouault, with your kind of painting..." and Desvallières told the prospective family, "He's a strange customer.."? "Be yourself, and even exaggerate a little," counselled Baignières.

On 27 January, 1908, Rouault married Marthe le Sidaner. She was the second youngest of a Breton family, whose father, a deep sea skipper, died when his youngest daughter was only a few months old. Their penniless mother brought up the nine children by giving piano lessons.

The two obstinate ones (1941)
Gouache for "Divertissement"

Private collection

Dancers (1941)
Gouache for "Divertissement"

Private collection

Her daughters were dutiful and unselfish. They had a lofty idea of moral duty, but in the matter of painting, their culture — that of their environment at that epoch — was less than mediocre. Henri le Sidaner, their brother, a painter who followed a very different line, told them, "What Rouault does is very powerful" but they could not appreciate either the work or the human value of a being of whom they knew nothing except the rumpus caused by a very vulnerable character. That was why, when he came, once a year, my father "withdrew into his shell", suffering from being misunderstood, unrecognized and not warmly welcomed. We were very fond of our grandmother and our aunts, but they felt we were so proud of our father, that the subject was never touched upon; that created a slight strain. Georges' dazzling conversations with his friends, the battle he waged for his art, his immense affection for his family, all remained unsuspected. Not, however, for the sister of my paternal grandfather, Aunt Amélie, who gave all that she had to the poor and lived like them; she understood my father and loved him with all her heart, as he loved her.

In speaking of our maternal grandmother, we called her "good-mother" — "bonne-mère" — "And what about mine?", exploded father. "Isn't she good?"

His fears on that score were groundless. Because she was less surrounded, left more to herself, we adored our grandmother. We were deeply grieved when she moved into a Home for the Aged in 1918.

In 1908, the young couple naturally set up home in the Moreau Museum, the first of our sixteen homes. I was born there.

> I can still hear the clear laughter
> Of my firstborn child.

Léon Bloy, whom my profoundly Christian mother understood at once, was a constant visitor, with many other friends.

"My call on Rouault lasted more than an hour," wrote Jacques Rivière to Alain Fournier, "I will tell you all about it and try to describe this extraordinary, ferocious man, full of great wrath and Christian, whom you feel to be so terribly strong." Jacques Rivière, Alain Fournier, André Lhote would join my parents on Sunday visits to the Louvre.

After a year, life at the Museum became impossible (troubles with the attendants, with the administration and so forth) and we had to move. My sister Isabelle was born in November, 1910 at 51 Rue Blanche, where my father's parents joined us.

"I am going to hold a show in December, so I am almost compelled not to take a holiday. It will have to be in the winter" — an illusion repeated annually — "But I am vexed for Marthe and the children. The worst thing is that I cannot persuade them to go without me... What would it cost to take a couple of modest rooms and a kitchen (furnished) for a month...? If my children need it, I should not hesitate... We have been very worried about Geneviève; I have been working with a great deal of anguish."

It was to Versailles that we went to get some fresh air. My mother gave a concert there which brought her a number of pupils. We therefore decided to move there, to 36 Rue de l'Orangerie. My grandfather, struck by a sudden stroke, was carried there by two removal men.

"My father died on Monday and today, now that I am no longer fighting against death, I find myself lost in a dark night, like a little child. I thought I was strong and here I am stricken down and crushed. I never had any communion with my father in the matter of art. He never talked about it, and I have a strong feeling that he never understood what I was doing... but secret and very loving fibres have snapped in me. This poor uneducated man had such humility, such gentleness, such goodness, right up to his last moments. I had a sort of feeling of discovering an admirable unknown or misunderstood work of art... My father was a silent man, and when I say 'he never talked about it and I have a strong feeling that he never understood what I was doing' I am judging like a feeble, blind man... What do we really know about what goes on in the minds of simple folk, who do not express themselves either in theories or in eloquent dissertations?"

My brother Michel, born two months later, inherited some of my grandfather's characteristics: "We shall celebrate the young man's birth together; we should be very happy if Madame Marguillier could come to the christening." She was godmother, Jacques Maritain godfather. "Do you like the name Michel? We hesitated between Gabriel, Stéphane and Jean-Marie, but the young gentleman's looks, in our opinion, go best with the name we have chosen. In the matter of beauty he is a cross between Duguesclin and a Negro boxer."

Without thereby dropping his old friends, who did not know each other, Rouault, attracted by the work and personality of André Suarès, seeking an answer to his doubts, confided fully in the writer from his very first letter: "At the moment, I am piously reading Dostoevsky's *Crime and Punishment*, in which I feel and discover new beauties every moment — and what unknown and marvellous beauties, in the midst of the most tragic and basest realities, transfigured by genius."

Is not the painter here throwing light on the whole meaning of his own work? Out of humility, he would have hesitated to claim this spiritual kinship with the great Russian writer, whose destiny was certainly more tragic; "... I am not a very great artist..."

"Unconscious of that capacity for fraternal devotion which he tried to dissimulate but which is proclaimed in his work," Rouault has that "fund of vigorous charity" which gives his work its unity, as it does to the work of Dostoevsky. They have many characteristics in common: vehemence, tenderness, vitality. In spite of their indignation at social injustices, both of them refused to allow their work to be used for political purposes.

Finally, veneration for Christ, as it dominates the work of the writer, was to dominate the work of the painter.

Roussalka (1941)
Gouache
for "Divertissement"

Private collection

As early as 1912, Suarès discerned the way which Rouault should follow: "You are coming out of a nightmare. May the New Year lead you to the serenity of light and the vision of peace." The painter expressed his gratitude: "You have had such a good and gentle influence in bringing me gradually out of the black melancholy in which I was plunged, without changing my basic nature, and I feel powerless to be any kind of help to you, but I am wholly devoted to you."

Suarès used to play the piano to us, while his wife, Betty, lively and very kind, sometimes used to exchange rather barbed words with my father, but only much later. "I hope I am not indiscreet in saying how happy I should be if Madame Suarès knew my wife. I am almost certain that she would be touched by my wife's simplicity, sacrifice and silent resignation. Madame Letellier was a very valued friend to Marthe and we shall always miss her."

My father used to go to Paris on Mondays for the Museum meetings, and fruitless approaches to publishers, to carry his heavy ceramics to Methey and call on his friends for advice. He himself also knew how to be receptive: "I stupidly talked about myself and about painting all evening; it is true that I did not know that your little Suzanne had been ill; if you want to give me great pleasure and to make up for my behaviour, we should be very happy, during this fine weather, if she would come and stay with us for a while, as long as you think fit; it would be some small way of thanking you..."

My mother went out to work all day: "More and more solitude at Versailles... never any communion at the right time. I certainly have a devoted friend, but he is even more overwhelmed than I am by interminable daily work." This "devoted friend" was Jacques Maritain. His gaiety and kindness, and those of Raïssa, her sister Véra and their mother, Madame Oumansoff, illuminated our childhood. They were our neighbours in the Rue de l'Orangerie, soon left for the Impasse des Gendarmes, where the house was not then divided up, as it is today; there was a garden, which no longer exists, and our walls oozed with damp.

It was there that a letter from Prague arrived one evening, immediately recounted to Suarès: "Miracles still happen... A man whom I do not know has decided that I should be a publisher and owner of my work... I have received a masterpiece of reproduction... He is a poor man... When I think that my album has been the rounds everywhere, and passed through the hands of rich and powerful men, enlightened art-lovers, it appears, and it has to be a poor Czech..." It was Josef Florian, his letters kept on coming, warm-hearted and full of children's drawings in exchange for ours.

On Sundays we used to have visitors and Father would become very animated. He used to write in the light kitchen, which gave on to the garden, but he worked in the loft-studio in a white dressing-gown; "your monk's habit", we called it.

When we came back from our many visits to hospitals, what gaiety there was in that kitchen where we ate our meals and took our baths! I recognized it, hardly changed, in the London exhibition, four years ago. It was there that Michel and I were sometimes serenely spanked — "it makes the blood circulate", confided Father, without any anger. It was there that he corrected my slate in the

Pierrot with bouquet
Gouache

Georges Rouault studio

Sketch for frontispiece
for "Les Fleurs du Mal"
Indian ink and gouache

Georges Rouault studio

evening, and that he got our satchels ready in the morning before taking us to school in the Rue Monboron. He still wore Gustave Moreau's overcoat, beneath the cape of which it was good to find his hand. In spite of disagreements, of dread of the future, torments and poverty — which we children hardly noticed — my father never let himself be defeated: "You good people of Versailles, you will never get the better of me!..."

Contact with Nature was a vital need for him: "The other evening, about eight o'clock, before dinner, I spent half an hour in the Park which I had not seen for three months, preferring the heights of St Martin or Jouy-en-Josas; the next day I completely re-did the series of landscapes."

Transposed landscapes, it is true, but in which I think I can recognize the Bassin de Neptune in *the Fountain*, the Allée des Marmousets in *End of Autumn* and the Grand Canal in the *Skating Rink*.

In August, 1914, the misfortunes of our country deeply affected my father. From St Efflam in Brittany he wrote: "This France, so much decried (sometimes by ourselves), is still in spite of everything, in this black and barbarous world, like a rare work of art... Above all the attachments of my heart and the ties of blood, my spirit is full of anguish... Oh, it is not fear, for a long time now I have rated life cheap. It is a quite different feeling and far above me, as though something very beautiful was about to disappear or might disappear."

And then on 1 September: "Miracle! I have started work again, in conditions you can well imagine, with nothing, in a little loft, just enough room to move..."

After a short stay with the Letelliers in Normandy, we came back. "My heart was so tired that, much against my will, I had to see a doctor. Either they don't have time to examine you properly or they do not know their business. When they are competent, they are invisible."

He knew how to do without them sometimes and he liked to look after us himself on the slightest cough, drawing marvellous landscapes on our back in iodine, lost for ever.

Our friend Professor Weinberg saw our shanty, the source of so much ill. "He advises me to cancel the lease — that is not so simple — I think it will be difficult for me to get out of it, since the landlord is himself a member of the Health Committee, which I have accepted as arbitrator." The landlord's name was Bonenfant, and he was the subject of a number of caricatures. "I unload all these troubles into my sketchbooks..."

During our last winter at Versailles, our little sister was born. My father had found a flat in the Rue Blomet in Paris where the baby fell seriously ill with toxaemia. "Our poor little Agnès, already so weak... ten days in hospital." She was returned to my parents pallid and lifeless, with a recommendation to try country air. In the train, my father laid her on his knees.

"But your baby is dead", asserted the other passengers, a cruel recollection, which haunted my father long after she was cured.

He never referred to it in front of Vollard, who once made the comment to him, "You are lucky to have children who bring themselves up on their own."

"A willing Prisoner"

In 1917 Rouault had shown 273 pictures.

Jacques Rivière, Coquiot, Apollinaire, Roger Marx and others had writen articles about him. The Colmar Museum had just acquired the *Child Jesus*. It was therefore with full information about the painter's reputation — he had been buying ceramics from him for ten years — that Vollard penetrated his studio. There he found 770 pictures which tempted him. The artist protested, "They are not finished!" — "All or none!" — "Very well, then, but on condition that I have the rest of my life to finish them."

This oral agreement was followed by the despatch of a cheque for 49,150 francs and the removal of the pictures. From then on, Rouault worked on them in Vollard's home. The dealer knew that he could only dispose of works which the painter judged worthy of his signature (in return for a very modest sum and a receipt). His heirs disregarded this clause and that was the origin of the proceedings which Rouault brought against them.

Vollard subsequently paid nearly two millions to supplement the 1917 cheque. Later, he bought some other pictures from my father at the "normal" price, which he was not slow to make known. In 22 years the dealer was to receive 563 signed pictures and 164 engravings from which he made large prints. Each painting or engraving therefore cost him on average less than 3,000 francs of the day.

But Vollard was a publisher, and Rouault had to cope with painting and engraving at the same time, with writing poems and articles "to relieve his heart", not to speak of his letters, sometimes veritable "epistolary explosions".

The wandering Jew (1934)   Gouache for "Le Cirque de l'Etoile Filante"
Private collection

"What can you expect,? I am not sufficiently devil-may-care, and the worst of it is that I take things too much to heart and I get on the nerves of people I want to be kind to..."

We were on holiday in the Yonne: "I miss Paris because of my work, but to talk seriously, would you like four dozen excellent new-laid eggs in exchange for some Indian ink?"

Vollard may perhaps have accepted the deal and, in answer to a suggestion of renting a house in Saumur to shelter his collection, he telegraphed "Suits me marvellously. You will look after the house." Derequisitioned by the Army Commissariat, the house was a veritable pigsty. Trailing his little family behind him, Rouault declared war on the bugs: "I have shed floods of paraffin, but the vermin have taken their revenge: they have bitten me."

These nocturnal discoveries, by candlelight alone, did not relieve him of painting: "I have just opened the parcels of paper; it is admirable...", or of the responsibility for hundreds of canvases of Renoir, Gauguin, Cézanne and Picasso.

Vollard brought work down and stayed to lunch at the house. He and I (aged nine) were reading the same picture papers: "Tell me," he asked, thoughtfully, "how do you think the serial will end?"

A young man in Saumur, who drew, was attracted to my father. André Girard liked him from the start, with all his heart. Rouault, who always avoided taking pupils, nevertheless gave him advice (as he did to Lhote, André Thomas, and later to Dalla Torre, and to many others). They went for long walks together, and André often came to joke with us. He remembered it all.

"Madame Rouault played a part in her husband's life which is rarely spoken of, the reader cannot imagine the strength of their love and their common spiritual life and the role it played in his artistic life... without her he might almost have lost hope. Her gentle, tranquil presence and her trust saved the sinking ship. But these moments of intimacy, these decisive points, had very few witnesses and she herself was so humble and modest that no one can imagine her talking about herself to a writer or even to an intimate friend." There followed a long correspondence and some coolnesses. One day, my father "spoke his heart out" in such terms that André complained, on returning home to his wife: "Ah, well," she said, "he was only treating you like one of his own children."

When the schools went back in 1918, we were at Versailles, Michel at the Lycée and Agnès out to nurse. My father went back to Saumur: "My wife writes me sensible but anxious letters on the cold, the heating and the lighting... She is not reassured to see me leading this fantastic Wandering Jew's life. I went off, I must confess, telling her I would be back in not more than two or three days... Here, I have worked well, I have tackled all the plates. You can bring the rest with you." "You" was Vollard, who had commissioned *Ubu* from him. Simultaneously, by agreement with the publisher, Rouault had undertaken *Miserere*. "During this winter and spring, I think I have broken the back of my fifty plates", which were, in fact fifty-eight, completed in 1927.

The Equestrienne
Gouache

Private
collection

Margot (1941)
Gouache
for "Divertissement"

Private collection

On 30 December, back in Paris at last! but homeless: "We can find nothing, in spite of all my looking. It is hard at my age, and in spite of my courage, to live in restaurants, hotels and boarding houses..."

For a while we lodged in furnished rooms in Versailles — but not in the same building — in the evenings we used to take Father the meagre meal served in our Institution, Mother carrying the milk-can full of soup. Jacques Maritain then lent us his Versailles flat, and two years later we finally joined up again at 20 Rue La Bruyère, Paris, in a minute three-room flat. We were all at boarding-school, the girls at Asnières, where Mother was now giving lessons, and Michel at Neuilly. Father worked on *Miserere* in his room in the mornings and lunched with Vollard to paint there in the afternoons, coming home late to dinner. In 1924 he lost his mother. She, too, always taking "other people's troubles" on her shoulders, effected a sort of transference, weeping over "those four poor children... Who will look after them... what will become of them?"

> Pearl of the purest water,
> The tender look of a vanished mother
> Still watches over me and consoles me
> In the desert of hostility,
> Indifference and negation.

It was from his mother that Rouault inherited a pronounced taste for removals. We had left Rue La Bruyère for Rue de Douai. In Vollard's attic there was a small bedroom and bathroom. Our removal induced my father to camp out there. But carried away by his passion for his art, bound by his commitments, he stayed there for five years, a "willing prisoner" in his own words. It was not without violent protest on our part. I cannot describe how greatly we missed him and how much he suffered.

Sometimes he came to dinner, entertaining his friends, like Marcel Arland, whose *Carnets de Gilbert* Rouault illustrated, and who, the first time he came, declared himself "a little surprised, and perhaps even a little annoyed to find Rouault attach so much importance to something so insignificant as the insults of a Mauclair." I can still remember that malicious article in which it was said, "Behind the epileptic you can sense the sham."

My father often spent Sundays with us, and always the holidays. He took my sister Isabelle away from school, where she was in the second class, and she became his Antigone. It was a good choice; energetic and gentle, she tried to calm him down.

"How shall I ever manage?" he cried in despair on arranging his canvases. "Why not try to finish even only four of them" she suggested. But no! he proposed to finish a hundred and thirty-three. And so there were more outbursts. Forty years later Isabelle still has nightmares about it. Sometimes she acted as go-between between her father and Vollard, between Vollard and Suarès.

In the spring of 1929, Diaghilev commissioned Rouault to do the decors and costumes for one of his Russian Ballets, the *Prodigal Son*. A month's relaxation at Monte Carlo. A series

Harlequin (1941)
Gouache
for "Divertissement"

Private collection

of pastels dates from this period, when he wrote: "Atlas bearing the world on his shoulders is a child compared to me... it is killing me... The whole of my effort, past, present and future, is at stake with Ambroise Vollard. That is why I exhaust myself with sleepless nights, why I pray in secret, it is perhaps why I shall succumb."

It was a real wrench for Rouault to part with a picture. Once the work was signed, it was a deliverance, a euphoria. "Take it away, don't let me see it again, hide it!" and we went off for a walk. Sometimes he would accompany my mother to choose materials or dresses for us.

Sometimes he would summon one or other of us and explain what he was doing, brush in hand. It was a privilege without any merit on the part of the young listener, for, as someone once said, "You would talk about Rembrandt to a ragman."

In the street as we walked along he would deliver monologues on Corot, Chardin, Degas. At the age of six I knew that Cézanne was a misunderstood genius. He detested "intellectuals", by which he meant those who put questions and made comments. He taught us to "look at Nature"; sitting in a square, he would reveal to me the beauty of a tree, or imperiously direct my eyes, which had strayed over the Château of Combourg, back to a simple patch of grass. He never struck us, but small objects would sometimes fly across the room.

We often used to play together, but he would never bow to the rules of the game, and the words imbecile or idiot were never very far off. When he was working he liked to hear my mother play Bach or Mozart or practise her scales. He often sang Gluck's *Orpheus* or Bach's *Pentecost*, or the *Two Grenadiers*, which he got from his friend Bischoff, Béranger's songs, or the students' songs of the College of Fine Arts. He liked to make us up, to dress up himself. We acted plays and they ended in squables. All the time he read aloud to us, The Gold-Bug, Flaubert's *Trois Contes*, Balzac, Villon, the Brontes. He knew La Fontaine by heart. I have never known anyone read so well, and I have never laughed so much. Exasperated by the radio programmes he bore down upon the set, unleashed a stream of insults and, disconcerted by our laughter, asked Michel, "Are you sure he didn't hear me?"

We would go to the Circus, the Comédie Française, the Œuvre. We saw Kafka's *The Trial* and Shaw's *Saint Joan*. Meeting Ludmilla Pitoeff he insisted on making her read the "Vrai Procès" of Joan of Arc, for which he had always had a fervent admiration.

Having been invited to a very good restaurant, he wanted us to taste the same savoury dishes, and booked a private room. We came in behind our parents, children from three to ten, in black velvet and lace collars. From the sympathetic looks of the head waiter, I understood how unusual was our visit.

Father himself used to cook for us: "The secret of my cooking?" he would say. "Let everything simmer gently".

We are sometimes asked whether as children we were embarrassed by Rouault's subjects. Absolutely not. We were not objective spectators set down "in front of" his work; we had grown up with it, we were impregnated with it, it was an integral part of our life, with all its characters. These are links which cannot be severed without amputation.

Great Expectations

In 1935, my father found an excellent flat with a studio in the Rue de Courty, Paris. The family transported its Lares and Penates, and he resumed his place while continuing his daily work in Vollard's studios, not far away.

"The nightmare of works which had been dragging on for more than twenty years" ended happily; thanks to Lacourière, *Le Cirque de l'étoile filante* and *Passion* were published in 1938.

The following summer, learning of Vollard's death in a motor accident, my father was deeply moved, and unable to walk; he had to send for Isabelle. The studios were placed under judicial seals.

When war was declared, we had not seen my brother, who was already serving with the colours, for a year.

Rouault had spent the month of August with a young Swiss — Claude Roulet — whom he had known for three years, a stay at Versailles which was a real relaxation. My parents left Paris, where Isabelle wanted to stay. Agnès and I spent the winter with them in the Sarthe. My father had brought a lot of work with him and his studio was well set up. In the evenings, by the fireside, he read us Dickens's *Great Expectations*. "I have been such a prisoner all my life", he mused, "that I have a nostalgia for travel."

The exodus, at my initiative, was a sad journey. Agnès would have preferred to wait for news of her husband, prisoner in a reprisals camp.

I had put the *Circus Girl* on the roof of the car and loaded up all the family: "I am a sedentary and they have made me a commercial traveller... instead of a secular I have become a restless soul..."

At the most tragic moment, when we were humiliated and overwhelmed by the misfortunes of our family, we brought my father a telegram, opened with pounding hearts. "Vive la

The Mocker (1941)   Gouache for "Divertissement"
Private collection

Decorative flowers
Gouache

Georges Rouault studio

France, now more than ever, Claude Roulet." It was unforgettable.

In the South, painting the *Aristocrat Pierrot*, the *Equestrienne* and *Divertissement*, my father thought sadly of his "lost children", *Christs*, *Legendary Landscapes* or *Biblical Landscapes*, some in the garret of Vollard's studios, others at the mercy of the occupying forces. Like my mother, he lost four stone. And yet, should we have stayed?

"We have had a narrow escape... I have also been visited by high grade iconoclasts (the S.S., installed in the house in the Sarthe). We have found everything, books, papers, paintings, in a terrible state... all knocked about, a veritable massacre."

Then came the return to Paris, and back to the Sarthe again: "The water no longer flows in the frozen pipes, and what will people say who have neither home nor heating?... neither soft beds nor supplies... a sad trade since 1938... the unfortunate Michel is writing his thesis under deplorable conditions..."

A letter from my father told me of his anxieties for Andrée Girard, who had been deported. He never breathed a word of it, dissimulating his cares and worries with a fanatical sense of modesty, thanks to his extraordinary vitality. At the age of 73, his conversation amazed his partners; never any incoherence but he was always leaping into digressions and parentheses and one had to be ready to reply immediately and briefly to his always unexpected "What was I saying?"

His first grandsons distracted him in their own fashion: "assaults, yells, constant romping, even during meals, when you get back there will certainly be planty of action..."

He promised them "chocolate cigars when Olivier II is weaned, and chocolate is obtainable again." Michel's three boys — Jean-Yves, Olivier I and Gilles — received letter after letter, even before they could read: "Help your mother, you young rascals... Have you made the marble disappear that the terrible Marie-Hélène (his first grand-daughter) nearly swallowed?"

About Agnès's baby, not yet talking: "We have Bernard, less loquacious than the honourable gentlemen in Parliament when it comes to pastis..."

To Father Régamey: "Father, pray for my four children, and my six rascals of grandsons."

More than ever he began to play the clown, and even the buffoon in public. "With this Residents' Examination," he told a complete stranger "Michel no longer bothers with me... If you only knew how they treated me here... Madame no longer mends my linen... Where is your idiot sister?..." The visitor noted, noted. When he had left, after some reproaches, we could not help all bursting into laughter: "I am the gayest dog there ever was on earth..."

Our cousin, André Thomas, took to painting. He spent some years in Paris and went back happily to Algiers, where he was accidentally killed.

With the arrival of fame, a new atmosphere was created; the "diabolic Rouault" was no longer "the horror painter"; people studied his complexes instead — it was all the fashion. "Baignières, always clear-sighted", wrote in 1934: "Quite in spite of yourself, you have won the respect of the snobs after the admiration of the real connoisseurs."

And yet, the shows and the criticisms of Cogniat, Lhote, Warnod, Vauxcelles, Salmon, Waldemar George, touched him. He was sensitive to the biographies of M. Puy and de Charensol, to the articles of Marcel Arland and his friendship. The lectures given in Belgium from 1927 onward by Georges Chabot — who, by his correspondence, became a dear friend — the 1937 Exhibition in the Petit Palais and the important work of Lionello Venturi, were all very good for him, as were the articles of Courthion, and, later, Dorival, and the lectures of Maurice Morel. His joy was nevertheless tinged with sadness:

"Everything people see in my painting was already there when I was forty. Why did people not seek me out then? Now, it is too late..."

He was still worried about the fate of his unfinished paintings, in the hands of the Vollard heirs, to which it was so easy to add a forged signature. After four years, relying on Maurice Courtot, who was to display as much heart as skill, Rouault resigned himself to legal proceedings: "I only wish I could disappear far away from these hateful disputes, which I am not made for..." Everything was certainly done to spare him from them.

"I feel, if I dare say so, in a more contemplative vein", inconsistent with the turmoil of a legal action of which my sister bore the brunt. Certain echoes of it nevertheless reached him: "Maître de Monzie, Lucien Vollard's counsel, treats me as an idle genius."

One fine day in 1947, thanks to Maître Baudelot and Maître Baraduc, the Tribunal recognized the moral right of the artist in his work. The proceedings had lasted four years: "If I had not had Isabelle, I should have gone mad..."

To celebrate the happy ending, we took my father to Switzerland and Italy, Isabelle, my husband and I, and the following year to Belgium and Holland. Delighted at finally seeing the works of art he had dreamed of since his youth, Rouault sang in the car all day long. "In the old days, Pierre Termier wanted to take me to Morocco... Here I am at 77 becoming a migrant bird..."

With the publication of *Miserere* on our initiative, he finally attained moral liberation, the "peaceful vision" reflected in the works of his last period.

It is my sister who will recount the last years of this incomparable father, to whom she had the great happiness of proving her love.

Thinking of the past, he would sometimes sigh: "How I regret my peaceful obscurity..."

Oh, peaceful obscurity, irradiated for us by your look, now turned towards the Light.

Versailles (the Terrace)
Gouache and oil

Georges Rouault studio

Self Portrait (1921)
Oil-paint thinned with turpentine

Georges Rouault studio